God's PROMISES for EVERY SEASON

warnerpress

305802100000523

Warner Press, Inc.

Warner Press and Warner Press logo are trademarks of Warner Press, Inc.

Written by: Julie Campbell and Robin Loisch

Cover and Layout by: Curtis Corzine

Printed in the USA

God's promises were not made just for one day, but for all time.

Praise be to the LORD....
Not one word has failed
of all the good promises he gave.

1 Kings 8:56 (NIV)

In a world that is forever changing, our God is forever the same.

From everlasting to everlasting you are God.

Psalm 90:2 (niv)

People in our lives may come and go, but God will never leave us.

God has said, "Never will I leave you; never will I forsake you."

Hebrews 13:5 (niv)

When we are at our weakest, God is at His strongest.

For Christ's sake,

I delight in weaknesses....

For when I am weak,

then I am strong.

2 Corinthians 12:10 (niv)

Trust is believing God not only can provide for our needs, but He will.

God shall supply all your need according to his riches.

Philippians 4:19 (KJV)

Your name is always on the heart of the God who loves you.

Do not be afraid.…
I have called you by name;
you are mine.

Isaiah 43:1 (nlt)

Even the smallest details are important to God.

Lord, you have made
the heavens and the earth
by your great power
and outstretched arm.
Nothing is too hard for you.

Jeremiah 32:17 (niv)

Someday God Himself will erase all pain and suffering from our lives forever.

God…will wipe every tear
from their eyes.
There will be no more death
or mourning or crying or pain.

REVELATION 21:3-4 (NIV)

Within each of us are gifts and abilities God can use to heal a hurting world.

You are the light of the world.
A town built on a hill
cannot be hidden.

MATTHEW 5:14 (NIV)

When we seek God, He will make Himself known.

You will seek me and find me
when you seek me
with all your heart.

JEREMIAH 29:13 (NIV)

No other rock
is as steadfast
and secure as
our mighty God.

There is none beside thee:
neither is there any
rock like our God.

1 Samuel 2:2 (kjv)

The God who created light cares deeply about your struggles.

My God turns my darkness to light.

Psalm 18:28 (niv)

We can lay
our burdens
at the feet of Jesus,
knowing He
truly cares.

Cast your cares on the Lord
and he will sustain you.

Psalm 55:22 (NIV)

The path ahead
may not always
appear clear,
but God is walking
before you.

We walk by faith, not by sight.

2 Corinthians 5:7 (KJV)

Peace comes,
not in avoiding trials,
but in turning
your fears over
to God.

Do not fear, for I am with you….
I will strengthen you and help you.

Isaiah 41:10 (niv)

In every season, in every situation, God is our refuge.

Trust in him at all times…
for God is our refuge.

Psalm 62:8 (niv)

Belief in God
is only the beginning
of life's greatest
adventure.

*Everything is possible
for one who believes.*

MARK 9:23 (NIV)

God is still writing your story. Trust Him with the next chapter.

Being confident of this,
that he who began
a good work in you
will carry it on to completion.

Philippians 1:6 (niv)

When we come seeking light and serenity, God will not turn us away.

God is light;
in him there is
no darkness at all.

1 John 1:5 (niv)

In God we find a safe haven of mercy, compassion, and grace.

Come to me,
all you who are weary
and burdened,
and I will give you rest.

Matthew 11:28 (NIV)

God uses our imperfections to more greatly reveal His glory.

My grace is sufficient for you, for my power is made perfect in weakness.

2 Corinthians 12:9 (niv)

Knowing Jesus
makes each day
something
to celebrate.

Blessed is the people
whose God is the Lord.

Psalm 144:15 (NIV)

God does not know the meaning of the word "impossible."

With God all things are possible.

Matthew 19:26 (niv)

Because of Jesus,

we are overcomers.

We are more than conquerors
through him that loved us.

Romans 8:37 (KJV)

We always have a home in the heart of our heavenly Father.

Those who know your name trust in you, for you, Lord, have never forsaken those who seek you.

Psalm 9:10 (NIV)

One moment spent in God's presence can make a difference that lasts a lifetime.

You make known to me
the path of life;
you will fill me with joy
in your presence.

Psalm 16:11 (niv)

While we may not see it, God's protection is all around us.

He will command his angels concerning you to guard you in all your ways.

Psalm 91:11 (niv)

Those who follow God today will know joy for all eternity.

The gift of God
is eternal life in
Christ Jesus our Lord.

Romans 6:23 (niv)

God is the healer of broken hearts and the mender of wounded souls.

He heals the brokenhearted and binds up their wounds.

Psalm 147:3 (niv)

If we choose to follow, God's light will always lead us to higher ground.

I am the light of the world.
Whoever follows me
will never walk in darkness.

John 8:12 (NIV)

In Jesus, we have a Friend who knows and understands what it's like to be human.

We do not have a high priest who is unable to empathize with our weaknesses.... Let us then approach God's throne of grace with confidence.

Hebrews 4:15–16 (niv)

Desert places are filled with hope when God is present there.

If I settle on the far side of the sea,
even there your hand will guide me,
your right hand will hold me fast.

Psalm 139:9–10 (niv)

Jesus doesn't want us to merely exist; He offers us a full and abundant life in Him.

The thief's purpose is
to steal and kill and destroy.
My purpose is to give them
a rich and satisfying life.

John 10:10 (NLT)

God knows you by name, created you for a purpose, and loves you with a passion.

I know the plans I have for you...
plans to prosper you and not to harm you,
plans to give you hope and a future.

Jeremiah 29:11 (NIV)

True freedom is found when we embrace our identity in Christ.

If the Son sets you free, you will be free indeed.

John 8:36 (NIV)

God's faithfulness does not change with the seasons, but endures forever.

His compassions never fail.
They are new every morning;
great is your faithfulness.

LAMENTATIONS 3:22–23 (NIV)

If we love God,
we can be confident that
He is working behind
the scenes for our good.

We know that God causes everything to work together for the good of those who love God.

Romans 8:28 (NLT)

The closer we cling to the Vine, the more abundant our harvest will be.

I am the vine; you are the branches.
If you remain in me and I in you,
you will bear much fruit.

JOHN 15:5 (NIV)

No matter how unseen you may feel, God always has you on His mind.

How precious are your thoughts
about me, O God.
They cannot be numbered!

PSALM 139:17 (NLT)

Yielding control to God is the key to contentment.

Trust in the L*ORD*
with all your heart…
and he will make
your paths straight.

PROVERBS 3:5–6 (NIV)

Keep your focus on God, and perfect peace is sure to follow.

You will keep in perfect peace…
all whose thoughts
are fixed on you!

Isaiah 26:3 (NLT)

God has a winning battle plan— trust Him and stay calm.

The L*ORD* *will fight for you;*
you need only to be still.

Exodus 14:14 (niv)

When we call on Him, God promises to hear our prayers.

In my distress I cried
unto the L*ORD*,
and he heard me.

Psalm 120:1 (KJV)

You will never regret replacing worry with an unyielding trust in God.

Look at the birds of the air…
your heavenly Father feeds them.
Are you not much more
valuable than they?

MATTHEW 6:26 (NIV)

God gave us the gift of the Holy Spirit, who comforts us with His supernatural peace.

He shall give you another Comforter, that he may abide with you for ever.

John 14:16 (kjv)

When we don't know which way to go, God will take us by the hand and lead us.

Your ears will hear a voice
behind you, saying,
"This is the way; walk in it."

ISAIAH 30:21 (NIV)